Girls

31 POSTCARDS FROM THE JAMES GARDINER COLLECTION

FOURTH ESTATE • *London*

First published in Great Britain in 1994 by
Fourth Estate Limited
289 Westbourne Grove
London W11 2QA

Copyright © 1994 by the James Gardiner Collection

The right of James Gardiner to be identified as the compiler of
this work has been asserted by him in accordance with the
Copyright, Designs and Patents Act 1988.

A catalogue record for this book is available from the British Library.

ISBN 1–85702–264–5

All rights reserved. No part of this publication may be
reproduced, transmitted, or stored in a retrieval system,
in any form or by any means, without permission in writing
from Fourth Estate Limited.

Printed in Hong Kong by Colorcraft Ltd

© 1994 James Gardiner Collection

Published by Fourth Estate Limited

WINNIE BROWNE. "LA KRAQUETTE."

© 1994 JAMES GARDINER COLLECTION

PUBLISHED BY FOURTH ESTATE LIMITED

© 1994 James Gardiner Collection

Published by Fourth Estate Limited

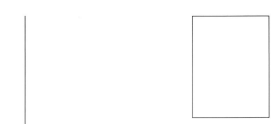

© 1994 James Gardiner Collection

Published by Fourth Estate Limited

MISS VESTA TILLEY.

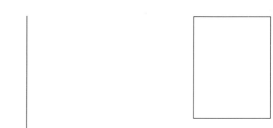

© 1994 James Gardiner Collection
PUBLISHED BY FOURTH ESTATE LIMITED

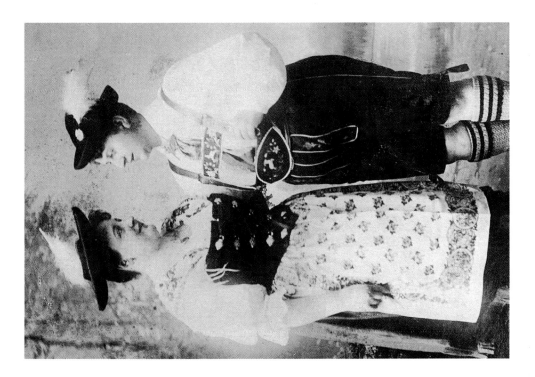

© 1994 JAMES GARDINER COLLECTION

PUBLISHED BY FOURTH ESTATE LIMITED

© 1994 James Gardiner Collection

PUBLISHED BY FOURTH ESTATE LIMITED

© 1994 JAMES GARDINER COLLECTION

PUBLISHED BY FOURTH ESTATE LIMITED

© 1994 JAMES GARDINER COLLECTION

PUBLISHED BY FOURTH ESTATE LIMITED

© 1994 JAMES GARDINER COLLECTION

PUBLISHED BY FOURTH ESTATE LIMITED

© 1994 James Gardiner Collection

Published by Fourth Estate Limited

© 1994 JAMES GARDINER COLLECTION

PUBLISHED BY FOURTH ESTATE LIMITED

© 1994 James Gardiner Collection

PUBLISHED BY FOURTH ESTATE LIMITED

© 1994 JAMES GARDINER COLLECTION

PUBLISHED BY FOURTH ESTATE LIMITED

© 1994 James Gardiner Collection
PUBLISHED BY FOURTH ESTATE LIMITED

M.me Rizzini - SAPHO

© 1994 James Gardiner Collection
PUBLISHED BY FOURTH ESTATE LIMITED

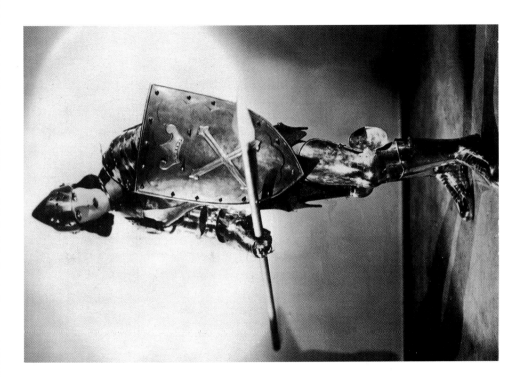

© 1994 JAMES GARDINER COLLECTION

PUBLISHED BY FOURTH ESTATE LIMITED

© 1994 James Gardiner Collection

PUBLISHED BY FOURTH ESTATE LIMITED

© 1994 James Gardiner Collection

published by fourth estate limited

© 1994 JAMES GARDINER COLLECTION

PUBLISHED BY FOURTH ESTATE LIMITED

© 1994 JAMES GARDINER COLLECTION

PUBLISHED BY FOURTH ESTATE LIMITED

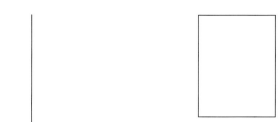

© 1994 James Gardiner Collection

PUBLISHED BY FOURTH ESTATE LIMITED

© 1994 James Gardiner Collection

PUBLISHED BY FOURTH ESTATE LIMITED

Vulcana, the Muscular Beauty

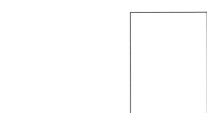

© 1994 JAMES GARDINER COLLECTION

PUBLISHED BY FOURTH ESTATE LIMITED

© 1994 James Gardiner Collection

PUBLISHED BY FOURTH ESTATE LIMITED

© 1994 James Gardiner Collection

PUBLISHED BY FOURTH ESTATE LIMITED

© 1994 James Gardiner Collection

Published by Fourth Estate Limited

© 1994 JAMES GARDINER COLLECTION
PUBLISHED BY FOURTH ESTATE LIMITED

© 1994 JAMES GARDINER COLLECTION

PUBLISHED BY FOURTH ESTATE LIMITED

Josephine Baker

© 1994 JAMES GARDINER COLLECTION
PUBLISHED BY FOURTH ESTATE LIMITED

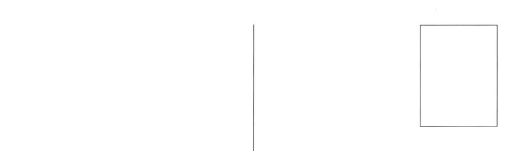

© 1994 James Gardiner Collection

Published by Fourth Estate Limited